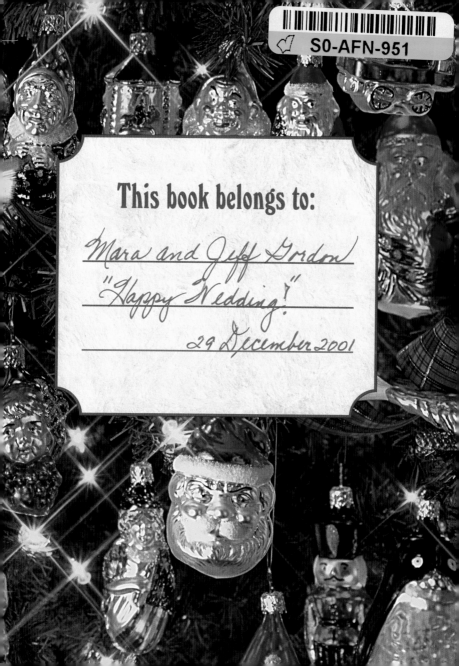

This book belongs to:

Mara and Jeff Gordon
"Happy Wedding!"
29 December 2001

Design & Layout:
Beth Merck, Chris Stevens

ISBN 0-9648534-1-8

Copyright © 2000 Merck Family's Old World Christmas®

Merck Family's Old World Christmas®
P.O. Box 8000
Spokane, WA 99203

Printed in U.S.A.
First Edition

Christmas Ornament Legends

Our Second Collection of Stories, Traditions, and Folklore from

The Merck Family's
Old World Christmas®

This book is dedicated to our children,
Jonathan and Katherine. May they preserve these legends
and keep the joy of Christmas in their hearts.

Old World Christmas®

An Heirloom is Born —
The Making of a Glass Ornament.

The natural beauty of a glass ornament embodies the laborious process of its creation. The steps involved in creating tomorrow's glass heirlooms are indeed numerous, but are exactly as they were years ago. These skills have been perfected and passed down from generation to generation in the authentic tradition of creating genuine, cherished Christmas heirlooms. Gifted artisans represent a living legacy to the exceptional talent and dedication needed to create tomorrow's heirlooms today.

Each glassblower begins with a "blank", a small hollow ball of glass with a long stem. Heated over a flame until it is red hot, the blank is set into the bottom half of a porcelain mold and then covered with the top half. The glassblower then blows in the stem until the molten glass conforms to the shape of the mold. He then removes the ornament, reheats it a second time and gives the stem one final puff. This extra step tempers the ornament, thereby preventing stress cracks.

Once the ornament has cooled, it is silvered. A mixture of silver nitrate, ammonia and distilled water is poured into the ornament along with a few drops of a combination of saltpeter, sugar and more distilled water. The ornament is then dipped into a hot water bath where the muddy-brown mixture magically turns into a glistening silver color. When rinsed, the ornament is placed upside down on a nail and set in a drying oven.

After completely drying, the silvered ornament is taken to the artist's table for painting. Applying each individual color is a separate process, and the ornament

4

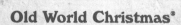

is repeatedly set aside to dry before the next color may be added. This can involve up to thirty applications and requires much skill on the part of the artisan to ensure exacting detail and that one color does not overlap another.

Glitter is then applied to the ornament to add sparkling highlights, the stem is broken off, and the cap is put into place. An heirloom is born and the radiant new ornament takes its proper place on the Christmas tree to offer its exquisite beauty to Christmas celebrations for generations to come.

Produced in limited quantities and exclusively imported by the Merck Family's Old World Christmas, these dazzling, delicate and affordable collectibles are treasures you and your family are sure to enjoy as part of your Christmas memories and traditions.

Bring the joy and magic of a traditional, old-fashioned Christmas to your home with authentic figural glass ornaments from the Merck Family's Old World Christmas.

Old World Christmas®

The Story of a Legend

Storytelling has long been an integral part of German culture. German people have always been fond of tradition and are very protective of their heritage, particularly surrounding the celebration of Christmas. Often credited with introducing the Christmas tree to the world, the German people's stories and holiday customs are the foundation of the legends that accompany many of the Merck Family's Old World Christmas ornaments.

Centuries ago, in tiny villages throughout the German countryside, parents amused their children on cold wintry nights with the telling of magical stories and fairy tales. These stories, often repeated many times over the years, became an inherent part of the children's lives and memories. As they grew, they too passed these stories on to their own children, creating a legacy of cultural pride and family traditions. As dialects and accents varied from village to village, so did traditional family legends, yet each tale was treasured by the family who told it.

The Merck Family's Old World Christmas first introduced Christmas ornament legends to American collectors with the whimsical story of the pickle ornament. The tradition of hiding a pickle ornament in the tree was first discovered by Tim and Beth Merck while visiting a small village in Germany. The contagious merriment and delight of the old woman telling the story was a feeling Tim and Beth wanted to share with families in the United States. Additional visits to other villages and conversations with German families eager to share their fond Christmas memories uncovered a wealth of Christmas traditions, ready to be shared with the world.

The Merck Family's Old World Christmas takes great pleasure in providing an opportunity for today's collectors to share the same magical legends with their friends and families during the holidays through this collection of Christmas ornament traditions.

Old World Christmas®

Garlic, that tasty, pungent herb, has been used for centuries as a flavorful spice and a miraculous healing drug. Used by Samarians, Hebrews, Egyptians, Greeks, Romans and every known civilization since, garlic is credited with various powers such as neutralizing a scorpion's sting, curing earaches, increasing bravery in soldiers and warding off vampires. Garlic is still eaten as a savory, healthful herb that is good for the heart. The lifelike garlic ornament, lacking only in smell, carries a good health blessing to the home of every tree it adorns.

Snowmen have always been children's special friends. A time long ago, when toys were scarce and the closest neighbors could be miles away, children looked forward to the year's first snowfall with great anticipation. Snow, this wonderful gift from heaven, afforded children a chance to go sledding, but even more exciting, it gave them the opportunity to create a new companion – their very own snowman! Each of the jolly fellows had its own distinct expression and "life expectancy." With a carrot from the pantry, coal from the furnace, twigs from the yard, an old hat, and perhaps a pipe borrowed from Grandfather, a child would build a snowman. Their friend of snow would disappear when the weather warmed, but would live on in childhood memories.

Robins have been associated with Christmas for ages, for it was on this occasion years ago that it acquired its red breast. According to legend, the robin's heart ached to see the Christ Child shivering as the fire began to die. The bird flew close to the embers and began fanning them with its wings. The flames grew and the fire soon burned brightly. The heat had turned the compassionate robin's breast red.

Turn-of-the-century Christmas cards frequently depicted the colorful robin's image, often surrounded by sprigs of holly and other holiday greenery. Today, the robin ornament is traditionally clipped to a prominent bough of the tree to remind us of its selfless compassion and commemorate its important role in the Christmas celebration.

Old World Christmas®

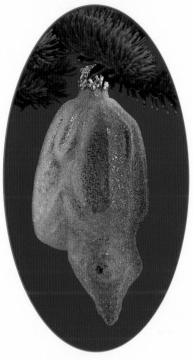

Frogs have long been considered a symbol of good luck in business. Since a frog can only travel forward, he is always progressing, representing a prosperous future. For this reason, the frog ornament also symbolizes best wishes for the future, so it is often given as a gift at graduations, weddings, or upon leaving home, as well as a special gift when beginning a new business venture. The forward-looking frog is an essential element of any well-dressed tree.

𝖂 atch Birds are shown on early Christmas postcards, books, and chromolithographs accompanying St. Nicholas. Colorful songbirds are perched on his shoulder, staff, or at his side. They have come to report what they have seen. They have flown throughout the villages and towns and have watched the children to see if they have been good. So, before Christmas, cheery glass bird ornaments are placed throughout the German home as "Watch Birds." Children are aware that the birds are Santa's special friends who monitor and report back to him whether or not they have been good little boys and girls. These bird ornaments most often evoke nostalgic memories of Grandma's tree and past family Christmases.

Turnips must be planted by naked gardeners according to an old English wives tale. Perhaps the old women chuckled at the yearly spectacle of naked gardeners, or more likely, they knew that if turnips were planted too early when the soil is still cold, they will grow into woody stalks and bolt to seed without developing into tender, crisp, rounded roots. So if the temperature and the soil are warm enough for the gardener to run around and plant undressed, the turnips are much more likely to thrive, according to the gardener's old Farmer's Almanac.

Pinocchio was first created by Carlo Collodi in Florence, Italy in 1881. This classic tale of a mischievous wooden puppet continues to delight children around the world. What child could fail to identify with this exuberant puppet who tries so hard to be good, but is so often overcome by longings for excitement and the urge to misbehave? Even before Geppetto, the old crusty carpenter, finishes carving him, Pinocchio is already teasing and poking fun at his creator. Geppetto's patience is rewarded later when Pinocchio finally learns from his own experience that it is wise to follow good advice from those who love you. The legend of Pinocchio's changeable nose as a barometer of truthfulness is well known, nevertheless, the moral of this tale continues to elude many to this day.

The Fox and Goose are the central characters in a well-known German fable, which is popular throughout the entire year. While riding across town on a wooden cart, a young goose glimpses the alluring city life. Upon returning to her farm, she dreams of the excitement and glamour of the city, while her brothers and sisters receive lessons in swimming, marching, and laying eggs. The silly goose tricks and exploits other barn animals in order to create a costume for herself consisting of a straw hat, veil, high heels, and fake eyelashes. After parading through the barnyard, she wanders into the woods where a fox flatters her, tricks her, and then prepares to kill her. She manages to escape only with the help and cooperation of the barnyard animals. The tale of the fox and goose warns us to resist the temptations of glamour and materialism, which can detract from the peace and joy of Christmas, and value our true friends and home.

Christmas Carol

In Charles Dicken's treasured classic, "A Christmas Carol", Ebenezer Scrooge is associated with greed and selfishness because he has allowed his wealth and material possessions to control his life. At the stroke of midnight on Christmas Eve, a series of visits from the Ghosts of Christmas

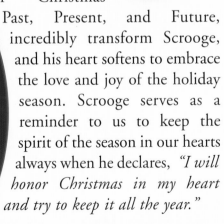

Past, Present, and Future, incredibly transform Scrooge, and his heart softens to embrace the love and joy of the holiday season. Scrooge serves as a reminder to us to keep the spirit of the season in our hearts always when he declares, *"I will honor Christmas in my heart and try to keep it all the year."*

Marley's Ghost from Charles Dickens' holiday tale, "A Christmas Carol," represents the result of a life squandered by not understanding true meaning of Christmas. This haunting character warns the greedy and hard-hearted Scrooge to repent the error of his ways and learn to embrace the qualities of mercy, benevolence, and the joy of giving before it is too late. This finely-crafted ornament serves as a reminder to us all to share happiness and to be generous at Christmas and year-round.

Old World Christmas®

Gingerbread House ornaments depict one of the favorite traditions of the holiday season – sweets! Christmas festivities have always included special foods and certain cookies and candies are made only at this time of year. One of the most beloved holiday confections is the gingerbread house. The tradition of sweet, flavorful, spicy gingerbread signifies the remembrance of the precious spices brought to the Christ Child as a gift from one of the Wise Men.

Contests were held in small villages in which women and children competed to create the most elaborate and realistic building made entirely out of gingerbread, candies and sweets. Often, replicas of the village church, homes or local landmarks won first prize. Following the awards, everyone gathered around to gobble up the tasty creations.

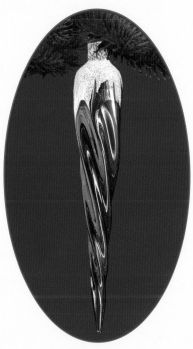

Icicles are a nostalgic reminder of a story which legend says took place on a cold December night long ago. As a snowstorm raged throughout the forest, a little child seeking shelter crept under the thick, strong branches of a sturdy fir tree. He remained protected there until the storm had passed. The next morning the grateful child thanked the fir tree. After learning that it had been the Christ Child who had been kept safe under its branches, the fir tree wept with joy. The fir tree's tears froze upon its boughs as icicles, which glistened and shone in the bright winter sun.

Bees were thought by Ancient Egyptians to have sprung from the tears of the sun god, Ra. This was because a bee's sense of direction is based on the position of the sun. Bees were also seen as givers of life, since they seemed to die in late fall, but always returned in the spring.

Another legend from ancient Rome tells the story of a bee that took some of its honey as a gift to the god Jupiter, who was very pleased and offered a gift in return. The bee asked for a stinger to help it protect its honey. Although Jupiter agreed, he decreed the use of the stinger would cost the bee its life, so it would be used only when necessary.

Today, as bees must work together to make honey in the hive, the Bee ornament reminds us that industriousness and teamwork are necessary to achieve great rewards.

Old World Christmas®

𝕿he Christmas Spider legend tells of an old woman who was busily cleaning her home Christmas Eve – the day the Christ Child was to come and bring blessings. When she retired for the night, her home was spotless – even the spiders had been banished to the attic. But the tiny spiders, eager to see the tree, crept back out into the room. They explored the entire tree, but as they did, they left lacy cobwebs over the surface of the tree. When the Christ Child came to bless the tree, he was surprised to see the tree covered with cobwebs. He knew how hard the old woman had worked to clean the house, so he touched the webs and they all turned to sparkling silver and gold. Ever since, Christmas trees have been hung in tinsel, and it is considered good luck to have a spider among the decorations on your tree.

Ornament Legends

Horns were an integral part of old-fashioned Christmas celebrations. According to legend, loud noises frightened evil spirits who visited during the winter solstice. Traditions and festivals focusing on noisemaking were popular during the holidays. Firecrackers, guns, cannons, and horns were the principal noisemakers. In the 19th century, horns played an indispensable role in American Christmas celebrations. Bands of horn-players paraded through streets till early hours of the morning banishing all sorrow and welcoming Christmas. Horns of every size and shape existed, including special horns resembling fish. With the increasing popularity of heralding in Christmas with carols, horns remain a powerful instrument in proclaiming the joyous season.

$\mathfrak{C}$hampagne is considered a lucky wine. In fact, the ritual of launching and christening a ship would not be complete without a bottle of champagne. The significance of the smashed bottle and flowing wine comes from an old ghastly and superstitious ritual that demanded a blood sacrifice to the sea gods to ensure the safety of the ship and its sailors. Breaking a champagne bottle across the bow of the ship as it is launched brings good fortune to the ship and all those who sail on it, provided that the ship's name is not changed.

The champagne bottle, the cork, and the wine itself all have connotations of good fortune, so the Champagne Bottle ornament is chosen to celebrate almost any special occasion, including childbirth, baptism, and marriage.

Old World Christmas®

Black cats are featured in an old Norse legend that tells the story of Freya, a goddess who rode a chariot pulled by black cats. The cats served Freya faithfully and as a reward, after seven years, they were turned into witches. This tale led to the superstition that all cats were the familiars of witches, or witches in disguise.

There were other black cat superstitions, too. In Europe, if a black cat crossed your path, it was thought to be unlucky. If it walked toward you, it would bring good luck. An old common belief was that black cats had special gifts. Cats could foretell the future and see spirits that humans could not. For this reason, black cats were often kept on ships as lucky mascots.

Old World Christmas®

Poinsettias represent the pure joy of truly selfless giving at Christmas. On Christmas Eve, a young boy knelt in prayer before the altar in his village church. Although he was penniless, he fervently wished that he had something to give the Christ Child for His birthday. Since the small boy's devotion was so sincere, a miracle occurred which allowed him to give something that no amount of money could buy… a brilliant red flower that sprang up at his feet. It was to become known as the Flower of the Holy Night.

The American ambassador to Mexico from 1825 to 1829, Dr. Joel Roberts Poinsett, was very interested in botany and brought back this unusual and beautiful plant to his home in South Carolina. With its bright red and green foliage, it became a popular holiday plant and was re-christened the Poinsettia in honor of the ambassador.

Ornament Legends

Dolphins are nature's ambassadors. Dolphins seem to have reversed the law of the wild, seeking humans, rather than fleeing from them. Throughout history, many tales of dolphins saving humans from drowning, befriending them, and then carrying them on their backs have been recorded. Pliny, the Roman historian, tells of a wild dolphin taking a boy for a ride. In Ancient Greece, killing a dolphin was a crime punishable by death.

Today, reports of wild dolphins coming into bays and inlets in order to make contact with humans are not uncommon. Those who encounter the playful and gentle dolphin often describe feelings of love and friendship that seem to emanate from this marine mammal. Some people believe that dolphins radiate a positive energy, which rebalances and heals.

Old World Christmas ®

edgehogs are beloved little creatures, both in the wild and as pets. Farmers have long been delighted with these tiny animals since they are helpful in keeping many pestilent bugs in check. Children still marvel at the changes of the darling hedgehog's coat. His coat feels soft when he is gently held in one's hands and stroked, and yet when he is frightened, he quickly turns into a prickly ball. So, the Hedgehog ornament reminds us to be gentle and kind to others and they will return the favor.

𝕮andles traditionally play an important part in Christmas celebrations. Ancient Romans lit candles during the heart of winter to drive away the evil spirits of cold and darkness. Light symbolizes rejuvenation and rebirth. Moravians believe that the candle symbolizes the sinless body of Christ and the wick represents His spirit. A lit candle symbolizes Christ as the Light of the World. The traditions of Christmas Eve candles began in 1747 in Marienborn, Germany. Bishop John de Watteville sought a way to illustrate the mystery of Reincarnation to children in his parish. He explained that the flame represents the light of Christ's love because the Savior died for humanity. Today

Christmas Eve worshippers take candles home with them to signify the responsibility of Christians to take the light of Christ out into the world. Candles in the windows of homes during Christmastime are said to light the way of wanderers in search of the Christ Child. As symbols of generosity, purity, and goodwill, a candle in the window welcomes weary travelers during the winter holidays.

$\mathcal{P}$ineapples symbolize graciousness and friendship. Colonial sea captains returning from tropical voyages would take pineapples from their ships' cargo. They hung the pineapples on their front doors or gateposts as signs of hospitality and welcome. People eventually began carving designs of pineapples into their doorways to welcome friends or even strangers into their homes. Hanging from the Christmas tree, pineapples, with their exotic sweetness and unique shape, greet family and friends as they join together in the holiday festivities.

Old World Christmas®

Edelweiss is a delicate white flower which grows in the high rocky soil of the Alps. From the small villages at the base of the Alps, young men climb to great heights on the mountains to reach the tiny flowers and pick one for their beloved. Their climb is sometimes dangerous and difficult. The gift of an edelweiss flower is proof of the climb and an indicator of the strength of their love. The gift of an Edelweiss ornament is meant to signify true love, which will withstand and overcome any perils in its way.

Ornament Legends

℘**olar Bears** were thought to be ancestors of the Lapps, according to an old legend. The people called the bears "grandfather." In the northern lands, the polar bear was king of the beasts because it was large, swift, supremely powerful, and a deadly killer of men. Since the Arctic people often wore clothing made from sealskins, when the polar bear picked up their scent, they smelled of sealskin and the bear mistook them for seals. Today, the polar bear has a more benign association. He is often considered to be one of Santa's friendly neighbors.

Panda Bears once had pure white fur according to ancient legend. One of the Panda's best friends was the youngest girl of four sisters and they often laughed and played together. One day a hungry tiger crept up on them. The tiger was about to eat the panda, when the young girl rushed to stop the attack and was instead killed herself. The panda was so distressed that it rubbed black ashes on its arms and legs as a sign of mourning and cried for a long time, rubbing its eyes with its paws. From that day onward, the panda has had black rings around its eyes.

Until AD 2, the panda was considered rare and semi-divine in China. From 06 BC to AD 24, Chinese emperors kept rare beasts in the palace gardens and the most treasured of these were the pandas. The Chinese poet Bai juyo wrote that the panda had magical powers that could ward off evil spirits and natural disasters and prevent disease.

Old World Christmas®

Owls are considered to be symbols of wisdom, seeing through the darkness of ignorance because they can see in the dark, and look thoughtful and serious.

In modern western culture, the owl is also linked with ghosts and dark forces. This is probably because most owls fly primarily at night, flitting about silently and letting out occasional mournful hoots.

The owl's hoot has many superstitions attached to it. In some areas of rural France, it's thought that if a pregnant woman hears an owl hoot, she will have a baby girl. In ancient Rome and in Celtic lore, an owl that hooted at the time of death was believed to be waiting for the soul of the dying person. An old English belief held that the screech owl only called when rain was on the way.

Ornament Legends

$\mathfrak{C}$hristmas trees date back to the 8th century when a group of Germans who were about to sacrifice a child to Thor were stopped by St. Boniface. The sacrifice was taking place under an oak tree, so St. Boniface cut down the oak, revealing a small fir tree, which he proclaimed a symbol of Christ and the spirit of love that Christ tells.

Another early legend tells that Martin Luther created the first Christmas Tree. One Christmas Eve, he went for a late walk through the forest. Inspired by the sparkling, snow covered trees reflecting moonlight and the twinkling stars showing through the branches, he cut a small fir tree, took it home, and decorated it with candles.

The Christmas tree as we know it also descends directly from a representation of the Tree of Knowledge of Good and Evil in the Garden of Eden. It was featured in the traditional medieval mystery play performed on Christmas Eve within a circle of lighted candles. The re-enactment of the story of Adam and Eve culminated in their expulsion from Paradise. The play, however, ended optimistically with the promise of a savior sent by God who would be the incarnation of the Son of God. An evergreen tree was hung with apples and symbolized the temptation and fall of Adam and Eve. Because of the fir tree's use in these religious contexts, candles came to represent Christ, the Light of the World. In the early 19th century, the Christmas tree was widely accepted through-out Germany and Europe. Prince Albert, the German born husband of Queen Victoria, is credited with pop-ularizing this custom with the English.

Ornament Legends

Lighthouses are sources of inspiration and comfort, symbolizing Christ, the Light of the World. Psalm 119:105 reads, "Your word is a lamp to my feet and a light for my path." Christ gave guidance and direction, sacrificing His life for humankind. Lighthouses act as reminders of the lightkeepers' legacy of courage and selfless concern for others' welfare. Sturdy structures of ever-beaming light, lighthouses protect ships during tempests or dark skies, guiding them to safety. As beacons of light, lighthouses serve as powerful reminders of Christ's wisdom and remain a special part of holiday decorations.

Ornament Legends

TO MY VALENTINE

H**earts** have long been associated with love and also with Valentine's Day. This holiday is believed to be a continuation of a Roman tradition, the festival of Lupercalia. On this day, a young man would draw a scroll inscribed with the name of the young lady who was to be his sweetheart for the year. This pagan tradition was integrated with the Christian celebration of St. Valentine, the martyr who penned "your Valentine" at the bottom of a letter.

The heart is also a symbol of the love of Christ, whose birth we celebrate at Christmastime. The glass heart ornament is the perfect combination of these celebrations.

Ornament Legends

Heart with Rings ornament is a combination of symbols and meanings. In addition to the heart shape, which is a symbol of love, two golden rings have been added. During a wedding ceremony, rings are lovingly exchanged as an outward sign of fidelity and true devotion and symbolize the trust between the two givers. The form of each ring is round and without end, so the rings symbolize mutual and everlasting love. The Heart with Rings ornament is the perfect gift for a wedding or anniversary.

Old World Christmas®

Christmas Roses come from the legend of the little girl of Bethlehem who followed the shepherds who had received the angels' message and were journeying to the stable. All the shepherds had gifts for the Christ Child, but the little girl had no gift to give. Weeping from sadness, she lagged behind the others. Then there appeared an angel in a glow of light who miraculously turned each of her tears into beautiful roses. Eagerly the little girl gathered them in her arms and laid them at the manger as her gift to the Lord Jesus.

Swans have been seen through the ages as symbols of purity, grace, and beauty, as well as loyalty, nobility, and courage. The loyalty and faithfulness of swans are both legendary and real – they mate with the same partner for their entire lives. Swans show tremendous courage when protecting their young and will attack anything they see as a threat. Because swans mate with the same partner for life, a swan's feather sewn into a groom's pillow by his bride was said to enlist the help of the gods and make sure that the groom remained faithful.

Old World Christmas®

Teapots remind us of the mid-afternoon ritual of tea time with friends and family. While sipping tea, eating biscuits, and resting and renewing oneself, it is truly the friendships that are renewed and family connections that are celebrated. The Teapot ornament reminds us to rest and nourish the body and soul, as well as relationships. The Teapot is truly a symbol of genuine hospitality.

Wreaths, like Christmas trees, are a part of the ancient tradition of bringing evergreens indoors during the time surrounding the winter solstice as a symbol of life. Evergreens were thought to hold mystical powers because they continued to flourish in the winter when other trees stood bare. Certain evergreen species, such as holly, ivy, and mistletoe, bear recognizable fruit only in the winter - a triumph of life and fertility over the elements. The tradition of bringing evergreens indoors during the winter is a symbol of hope for a fruitful year to come.

Turtles, or tortoises, show that slow and steady wins the race in the story of the Tortoise and the Hare. Turtles are at home anywhere because they carry their homes on their backs. When threatened, most turtles can withdraw into their shells to protect themselves. Many tribal creation stories say that the Earth was born on the back of a turtle. Some Native Americans refer to North America as Turtle Island because their legends say that when the world was covered with water, the turtle plunged to the bottom of the ocean and brought the land up on its back so the people could have a safe, dry home. Turtle ornaments remind us of the security that our hearth and home offer.

$\mathcal{F}$ish are a thread connecting numerous stories in the Bible, and today their symbol returns the focus of Christmas to its religious origins. Fish signify Christ's miracles of feeding 5,000 people with only two fish and five loaves of bread and of the disciples' catching overwhelming amounts of fish in their nets. The apostles were referred to as "fishers of men", recalling their responsibility of discipleship in the world. Like Christ, fish provide nourishment and sustain life. The symbol of a fish epitomizes the messages of the Christmas season -- renewal of life, rejuvenation, and love.

Storks   One legend states that a stork visited the Baby Jesus, and when she saw him sleeping on a rude bed of straw, she plucked the soft feathers from her breast to make his bed more comfortable. Another legend says that once a thatched roof on which a stork was nesting caught fire. The stork sat over her young to protect them and beat the flames with her wings. When the fire was extinguished, the stork was black with soot and smoke burns, but her children were safe.

Storks are very protective animals. On hot days, they have been seen carrying water in their bills to give their young a drink. The white stork is said to bring new babies to parents. This legend may have begun because storks are seen around water and water is traditionally associated with fertility. It may simply be because storks take very good care of their young. Both parent storks incubate their eggs.

he Rooster, according to legend, has only crowed once at midnight – at the moment when Christ was born. Hence Spanish and Latin American countries call their midnight mass on Christmas Eve "Misa del Gallo", the Mass of the Rooster.

In Devonshire, England, an old tradition has it that on Christmas Eve, if a girl knocks on the door of a hen house and hears a rooster's crow in response, she will marry within the upcoming year.

Belznickel made Christmas Eve visits to children in the Pennsylvania Dutch region during the 1800's. His origin traces back to the Protestant Reformation when Catholic priests could no longer acceptably act as the central gift-givers of the holidays. Yet, it was still important for people, especially children, to receive rewards for their good behavior and suffer punishment for their mistakes. Dressed in a fur coat, mask, and wearing a long beard, Belznickel assumed the role of Gift-Giver and began knocking loudly on each child's door on Christmas Eve. He questioned children about their behavior and asked them to recite a poem or prayer. Despite his hearty laugh, Belznickel's presence created fright because he always knew exactly which children misbehaved. He carried a bag filled with treats and a handful of switches. Belznickel scattered the fruits, candies, nuts, and cakes on the floor. As all the children scrambled and bent over to snatch the treats, Belznickel spanked the naughty ones! Legends surrounding Belznickel remain today as a warning to unruly children.

Teddy Bears were originally inspired by a 1906 cartoon that depicted President Teddy Roosevelt's hunting trip in the Rocky Mountains. The President had refused to shoot a bear that had been tied up for him. The cartoon unintentionally popularized the bear by portraying him as tiny and helpless. Intrigued by the cartoon, Morris and Rosie Michtom created a stuffed bear cub for their gift store. The bears' popularity multiplied, and the Michtoms received permission from the President himself to mass-market the stuffed animals as "Teddy Bears". Today teddy bears, coming in various colors, shapes, and sizes, maintain their immense popularity among children and adults.

Lions symbolize strength, honor, and royalty. According to legend, a powerful lion awakened one night to a little mouse running up and down his face. The lion placed his huge paw on the mouse in preparation to devour him when the mouse begged for his life, crying, "Pardon, O King, forgive me this time and I will repay your kindness someday." The lion laughed at the idea of a little mouse helping him, but he let the mouse go. Shortly after, the lion was caught in a trap and tied to a tree. The mouse recognized the lion's roar and gnawed away the ropes to set him free. The mouse reminded the lion that even feeble creatures can help the King of the Beasts.

Candy Canes were invented in England in the 17th century. At that time, the government would not let people celebrate Christmas. So a candymaker made a hard white candy in the shape of a shepherd's crook, or an upside-down letter J, as a secret symbol of Jesus. The three thin lines represented the Father, Son, and Holy Spirit. The larger red stripe reminded the people of the life of Jesus given up for all mankind. The candy cane is a double gift...a sweet treat and a symbol of the true meaning of Christmas.

Santa Lucia was a beautiful maiden who lived in ancient Rome who refused to renounce her Christianity. For this, she was burned at the stake, and later named a saint. Because her saint's day fell on December 13th, and this was a time when the northern counties of Europe celebrated their winter solstice, the festivals were combined and became an occasion to light candles. This is marked by the arrival of Santa Lucia in Swedish homes. The youngest daughter is usually chosen to represent Santa Lucia. Dressed in a white gown and crowned with a green wreath with lighted candles, she brings the traditional breakfast of coffee and breads to her family while she sings Christmas songs.

Ornament Legends

Jack-o'-lanterns are a part of Halloween, a celebration which has its roots in the ancient Celtic festival of Samhain. At Samhain the souls of the dead passed to the netherworld as phantoms and fairies, witches and warlocks, and demons. They visited the living who provided their supernatural guests with food and lit bonfires in their honor. As centuries passed, the harvest festival was incorporated into Christianity and October 31st became All Hallow's Eve, or Halloween. According to legend, a clever blacksmith named Jack, traded his soul to the devil for seven years of prosperity. He tricked the devil by also secretly receiving three wishes from Jesus and Saint Peter. Jack wished that anyone who climbed his pear tree, sat in his chair, or climbed in his purse must remain there until he chose to release them. The devil visited Jack three different times. He climbed the pear tree, sat in Jack's chair, and even disguised himself as an insect in Jack's purse. Each time he visited, the devil was forced to give Jack seven more years of prosperity in return for his release from the traps. When Jack finally arrived to the underworld, the devil no longer wanted him around and sent him back to St. Peter. As he left, Jack grabbed a burning coal and placed it in the pumpkin he was eating. He used this as a lantern to find his way to heaven and to warn demons to avoid him. Today, Jack-o'-lanterns are still believed to frighten off evil spirits.

Snow Maiden stories originated in northern Russia. According to one legend, a childless couple wished for a daughter and their wish mysteriously came true when a little girl showed up on their doorstep. She laughed and played outside without the cold bothering her a bit. She became their good and dutiful daughter and brought them much joy, yet every night she disappeared into the snowy forest. When spring came, she bid them goodbye with a promise to return every winter.

Today, as the granddaughter of Father Frost, the Russian equivalent of Santa Claus, she is a popular part of New Year's celebrations. She is depicted with blonde braids and a long blue robe with white fur trim. She often accompanies Father Frost in parades and other New Year's events.

Ornament Legends

Pigs have long been considered lucky animals. The term, *Dickbauch*, meaning fat stomach, is still popularly used in Germany on Christmas Eve. According to tradition, those who do not eat well on Christmas Eve will be haunted by demons at night. So, a dinner of roasted pork on Christmas Eve is thought to fatten everyone up and prevent any evil, as well as serve as a portent for a prosperous upcoming year.

Old World Christmas®

Peanuts symbolize mystery since their shells completely hide their contents. Called "treasures beneath the ground," nuts are also associated with wisdom because their contents are compact, sustaining, and enclosed within a single shell. Long ago, families gathered together to decorate the tree with special handmade creations. Peanuts were wrapped in gold or silver foil and used as Christmas tree ornaments. Often they were wired into grape-like clusters or formed into small trees. During the Victorian period, hostesses would end a fine meal with salted and spiced nuts rather than heavier desserts. Peanuts continue to capture the simplicity of past Christmases, while also recalling the anticipation of the season.

Old World Christmas®

Reflectors, or indents, are produced without the use of molds. The glassblower creates a perfectly round ball, then one side is heated red hot and pressed against a pointed object or patterned tool. Throughout the process the maker must blow steadily into the ornament to create just enough resistance to the indenting, yet retain the ornament's shape. Only very skilled craftspeople can create such treasures out of delicate glass. Reflectors were one of the earliest ornaments made and continue to enjoy their popularity today. They are truly reflections of the Christmas spirit!

About the Authors...

Many years ago, Tim and Beth Merck owned a retail store in Spokane, Washington, in which they sold antiques imported directly from Europe. In 1975, during an antiques buying trip Tim and Beth made to Germany, they purchased a large assortment of Christmas decorations to sell in America. This new venture proved to be remarkably successful, and they had difficulty meeting the demands of collectors and dealers for these new-found treasures. They are now the proud owners of the Merck Family's Old World Christmas, a major importer of authentic collectibles, including figural glass Christmas ornaments. Beth, widely known as E.M. Merck, continues to design beautiful Christmas heirlooms and today her works have become critically acclaimed and known to collectors throughout the world.

Inspired by the heirloom figural glass decorations Beth's grandmother had on her tree, Tim and Beth traveled to all parts of Germany in search of these precious ornaments. Driving from village to village, and literally knocking on door after door in search of suppliers, Tim and Beth befriended many storytellers along the way who were eager to share bits of their heritage. Their twenty-five years of extensive travels and close associations with

the artisans who create the authentic quality ornaments have provided them with a wealth of knowledge. Tim, with his degree in European History from the University of Idaho, and Beth, who studied Fine Arts, Art History, and German cultural traditions at Pomona College, Gonzaga and Eastern Washington Universities and graduated with a degree in Fine Arts, were enthralled as they learned firsthand about the age-old traditions of the German people through family gatherings, business associations, holiday festivals and evenings sipping beer in quaint village pubs.

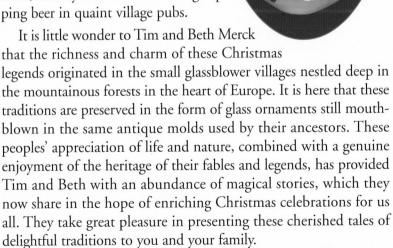

It is little wonder to Tim and Beth Merck that the richness and charm of these Christmas legends originated in the small glassblower villages nestled deep in the mountainous forests in the heart of Europe. It is here that these traditions are preserved in the form of glass ornaments still mouthblown in the same antique molds used by their ancestors. These peoples' appreciation of life and nature, combined with a genuine enjoyment of the heritage of their fables and legends, has provided Tim and Beth with an abundance of magical stories, which they now share in the hope of enriching Christmas celebrations for us all. They take great pleasure in presenting these cherished tales of delightful traditions to you and your family.

The Merck Family's
Old World Christmas Legend Index

The following is a listing of the Merck Family's Old World Christmas ornaments featured with the legends within this book.
There are many additional ornaments within the Merck Family's Old World Christmas collection which also represent these legends. Contact your favorite retailer for additional information.

Listed by legend, page number, item number, and the name of the ornament(s) pictured with the legend.

Old World Christmas®

Ornament Legends

A Joyful Christmas.